LADYBIRD HISTORIES

VICTORIANS

History consultant: Philip Parker
Map illustrator: Martin Sanders

A catalogue record for this book is available from the British Library

Published by Ladybird Books Ltd
80 Strand, London, WC2R 0RL
A Penguin Company

001

© LADYBIRD BOOKS LTD MMXIV

LADYBIRD and the device of a Ladybird are trademarks of Ladybird Books Ltd.

ISBN: 978-0-72327-729-3
Printed in China

LADYBIRD HISTORIES

VICTORIANS

Written by Jane Bingham
Main illustrations by Roger Wade Walker and John Dillow
Cartoon illustrations by Clive Goodyer

CONTENTS

THE VICTORIAN AGE

On 20 June 1837, a young princess became the new British queen. Her name was Alexandrina Victoria and she was just eighteen years old. Queen Victoria ruled for the next sixty-four years, until her death in 1901. During her reign, Britain became the most powerful country in the world.

A TIME OF CHANGE

By the 1800s, the Industrial Revolution had begun. New machines were invented and factories were built to produce goods at a higher rate than ever before. This time of dramatic change saw improvements in transport and a general move from countryside to town living.

The Industrial Revolution made Britain very rich, but it also caused social problems. In early Victorian times, workers in factories and mines suffered terrible conditions. Many people lived in poverty, and crime and disease were widespread. Fortunately, these problems were not ignored and reformers worked hard to improve people's lives.

THE AIR IN MANY VICTORIAN CITIES WAS DIRTY FROM THE SMOKE AND FUMES CAUSED BY FACTORIES.

THE BRITISH ABROAD

Queen Victoria ruled over an enormous empire. By the 20th century, the British Empire stretched across the world; from Canada in the north to New Zealand in the south. It covered a fifth of all the world's land, and included all of India, parts of Africa and Asia, and Australia (see page 14). Britain grew rich from trade within the Empire, but Victoria's army had to fight some fierce battles to gain land abroad.

GREAT ACHIEVEMENTS

The Victorians were great inventors, builders and engineers. Electric lights, telephones and even computers all appeared for the first time during Victoria's reign. Buildings were constructed all over the Empire and British engineers designed amazing tunnels, bridges and ships.

A famous name
The name Victoria is known all over the world. There are towns, lakes and waterfalls named after her, and there is even a Victoria railway station in London!

INTO THE NEW CENTURY

By the time Queen Victoria died, a new century had begun. In the 20th century, change happened much more rapidly than in Victorian times. But many of the changes that shaped our modern world started during Queen Victoria's reign.

YOUNG VICTORIA

Victoria was born at Kensington Palace, London, in 1819. She was the granddaughter of King George III, but nobody thought she would ever be queen. Her father, Prince Edward, was the king's fourth son and baby Victoria was fifth in line to the throne.

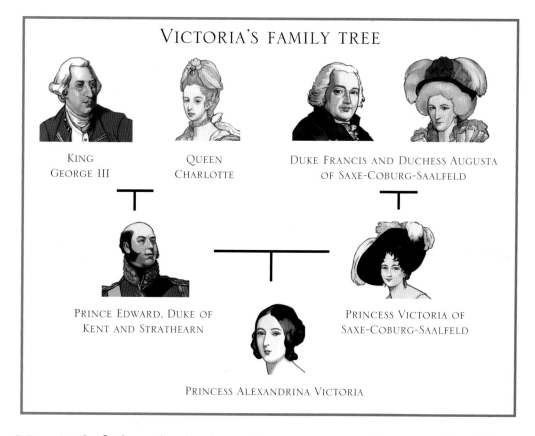

VICTORIA'S FAMILY TREE

KING GEORGE III

QUEEN CHARLOTTE

DUKE FRANCIS AND DUCHESS AUGUSTA OF SAXE-COBURG-SAALFELD

PRINCE EDWARD, DUKE OF KENT AND STRATHEARN

PRINCESS VICTORIA OF SAXE-COBURG-SAALFELD

PRINCESS ALEXANDRINA VICTORIA

Victoria's father died when she was just eight months old. She was brought up by her German mother, who kept a close watch on everything she did.

As Victoria grew up, she was taught at home by tutors. She did well in her lessons, but her favourite pastimes were painting, dancing and horse-riding.

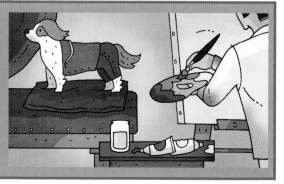

BECOMING QUEEN

By the time she was eleven years old, Victoria knew that one day she would be queen. Two of her uncles had died and her third uncle, King William IV, was in his sixties. In 1837, King William died and at the age of just eighteen, Victoria became ruler of Great Britain and Ireland.

Victoria was crowned in Westminster Abbey the following year. During the coronation, an elderly lord fell over, and Victoria helped him to his feet. The story of her kindness spread rapidly. The British people looked forward to the reign of a good and caring queen.

QUEEN VICTORIA HAD A NEW CROWN MADE FOR HER CORONATION AS THE ONE THAT HAD BELONGED TO PREVIOUS KINGS WAS TOO BIG AND HEAVY FOR HER!

VICTORIA AND ALBERT

Three years after she became Queen, Victoria got married. The British people hoped she would marry an English lord, but Victoria chose a German prince instead. Albert of Saxe-Coburg and Gotha was Victoria's cousin. He was handsome and clever, and she fell deeply in love with him.

A HAPPY FAMILY

Over the next seventeen years, Victoria and Albert had nine children – five daughters and four sons. The family spent most of their time at Windsor Castle, twenty miles west of London, but sometimes they headed south to Osborne House on the Isle of Wight or travelled north to Balmoral Castle in Scotland. Victoria, Albert and their children enjoyed simple pleasures, such as walking, riding and painting out of doors. In the evenings, they played games and sang around the piano.

MOST BRITISH PEOPLE SAW THE ROYALS AS THE PERFECT FAMILY.

A HARD-WORKING PRINCE

Prince Albert did all he could to help his wife in her work as queen. He acted as her advisor and took on many projects of his own. He worked especially hard to put an end to child labour, and supported British industry, trade and science.

A royal Christmas tree

Victoria and Albert helped to introduce the German custom of Christmas trees to Britain. In 1848, The *Illustrated London News* printed a picture of the Royal Family gathered around a decorated tree. After that, every family wanted a Christmas tree!

A SAD DEATH

Sadly, Albert fell ill and died when he was just forty two. The cause of his death was probably typhoid, a deadly disease that is carried in dirty water. Victoria was heartbroken.

Victoria hid away in grief for years after Albert's death. But the British public became increasingly resentful of her absence, and after ten years she took up her royal duties again. She reigned alone for forty more years, although she never really got over Albert's death and dressed in black for the rest of her life.

VICTORIA KEPT THE ROOM WHERE ALBERT DIED EXACTLY AS IT HAD BEEN WHEN HE WAS ALIVE. SHE EVEN TOLD THE SERVANTS TO LAY OUT FRESH CLOTHES FOR HIM EVERY MORNING!

RULING BRITAIN

Many important political changes took place in the Victorian era. The first trade unions were formed (see page 27) and the vote was extended to the middle and working classes. Women also campaigned strongly for their right to vote.

VICTORIA AND HER MINISTERS

There were ten Prime Ministers during Victoria's reign. When she first came to the throne, Lord Melbourne was Prime Minister. He soon became her great friend and mentor, teaching her about government. Victoria followed all his advice, though some of it made her unpopular with her people. Later, Prince Albert helped Victoria to be more independent and to stand up for what she thought was right, though she never interfered in politics.

GLADSTONE AND DISRAELI

William Ewart Gladstone belonged to the Whig party (also known as the Liberals). He wanted more power for Parliament and he campaigned to get more people interested in voting. Victoria disliked Gladstone because he lectured her on how the country should be run.

Benjamin Disraeli belonged to the Tory Party (also known as the Conservatives). He encouraged the growth of the British Empire and persuaded Victoria to take the title of Empress of India in 1876. He had charming manners and became a great favourite of the queen.

The ten Prime Ministers

1

VISCOUNT MELBOURNE
APR 1835-AUG 1841

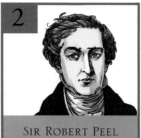

2

SIR ROBERT PEEL
AUG 1841-JUN 1846

3

LORD JOHN RUSSELL
JUN 1846-FEB 1852
OCT 1865-JUN 1866

4

EARL OF DERBY
FEB-DEC 1852
FEB 1858-JUN 1859
JUN 1866-FEB 1868

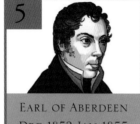

5

EARL OF ABERDEEN
DEC 1852-JAN 1855

6

VISCOUNT PALMERSTON
FEB 1855-FEB 1858
JUN 1859-OCT 1865

7

BENJAMIN DISRAELI
FEB-DEC 1868
FEB 1874-APR 1880

8

WILLIAM EWART GLADSTONE
DEC 1868-FEB 1874
APR 1880-JUN 1885
FEB-JUL 1886
AUG 1892-MAR 1894

9

MARQUESS OF SALISBURY
JUN 1885-JAN 1886
JUL 1886-AUG 1892
JUN 1895-JUN 1902

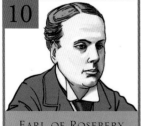

10

EARL OF ROSEBERY
MAR 1894-JUN 1895

TIME IN OFFICE
Some Prime Ministers were only in power for a few months, while others played a major role in running the country over many years. William Gladstone served as Prime Minister a grand total of four times! The dates below each name show each Prime Minister's time in office.

THE BRITISH EMPIRE

By 1900, Queen Victoria reigned over an enormous empire. The British Empire covered one-fifth of all of the world's land and contained a quarter of all the world's people. Countries in the Empire sold their goods to Britain and bought British goods in return. This global trade made Britain extremely rich.

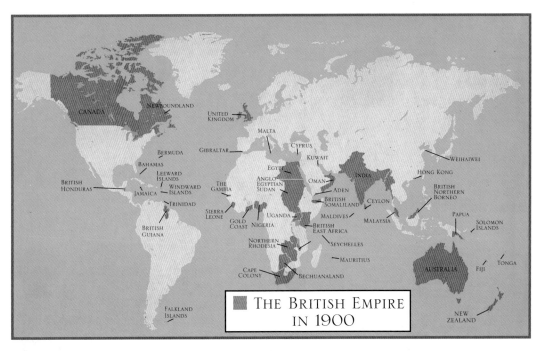

ON VICTORIAN MAPS, THE LANDS RULED BY BRITAIN WERE SHOWN IN PINK. RED WAS THE TRADITIONAL COLOUR OF THE EMPIRE BUT BLACK TEXT SHOWED UP BETTER AGAINST PINK.

BRITISH COLONIES

Colonies were countries that British explorers had claimed for their monarch. These then became countries of the Empire. Canada, Australia and New Zealand were all British colonies. Their people saw Victoria as their queen, even though they lived thousands of miles from Britain.

INDIA, AFRICA AND ASIA

In 1858, Britain gained control of India (see page 17). By the 1880s, the British also ruled parts of Africa and Asia. British merchants imported many valuable goods from these countries, including tea, spices, cotton, sugar and rubber. Cotton was especially useful to Britain. It was woven into cloth in the factories of northern England.

A BRITISH WAY OF LIFE

All over the Empire, the British built roads and railways, doctors and teachers set up hospitals and schools and officials travelled out to run them. Missionaries converted people to Christianity and children in many parts of the world learnt to speak English. However, not everyone in the Empire was happy to be under foreign rule and in some places there was resistance against the British.

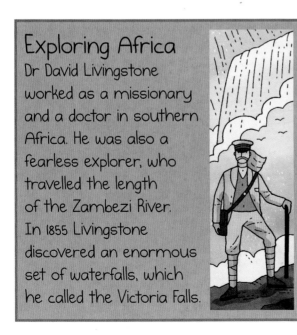

Exploring Africa

Dr David Livingstone worked as a missionary and a doctor in southern Africa. He was also a fearless explorer, who travelled the length of the Zambezi River. In 1855 Livingstone discovered an enormous set of waterfalls, which he called the Victoria Falls.

Tea time

Tea imported from India became a very popular drink in the Victorian period.

BRITAIN AT WAR

During Queen Victoria's reign, the British Army fought several wars to gain land for the Empire. The British also took part in the Crimean War. This terrible conflict was fought in the Crimea, a region between the Ottoman and Russian empires.

THE CRIMEAN WAR

War began when Russia tried to expand its influence into some Christian lands held by the Ottoman-Turkish Empire. Britain and France soon joined in the conflict on Turkey's side. The fighting lasted from 1853 to 1856. Tens of thousands of men were killed on the battlefields. Even larger numbers died from disease, cold and starvation.

WARFARE CHANGED DRAMATICALLY AFTER THE CRIMEAN WAR. THE USE OF RAPID-FIRE GUNS FROM THE 1860S ONWARDS LED TO MANY MORE DEATHS AND INJURIES THAN BEFORE.

THE INDIAN MUTINY

By the 1850s, the East India Company, a private British firm, controlled most of India and had a large army stationed there. This army included Indian soldiers (or sepoys), but many of them were angry with the British, as they felt that the commanders did not respect their religious beliefs. In 1857, this anger turned to violence. The sepoys led a rebellion against the British, with the support of some powerful Indian princes. In 1858, the rebels were defeated and the British government took control of India.

THE BOER WAR

Victoria's army fought several wars in Africa, but their fiercest struggle was against the Boers (Dutch farmers who had settled in Africa). After gold was discovered in South Africa, the British tried to seize land from the Boers. This resulted in the two Boer Wars, fought from 1880 to 1881 and from 1899 to 1902. The Boers fought fiercely, but in the end they were crushed by the much larger British forces.

AN INDUSTRIAL NATION

Britain became known as 'the workshop of the world' during the Victorian era. Most of the world's supply of iron, steel and cloth came from British foundries and factories. Britain also led the way in building machinery, railways and ships. As a result of this industry and trade, Britain became very wealthy.

COAL AND IRON

Britain's success as an industrial nation depended on coal and iron. Coal was burned in steam engines that produced the power to drive factory machinery. Smaller engines were used in trains and ships. Iron was used to make buildings and machinery. Iron could also be converted into steel, which was used to build bridges, railways, trains and ships.

TRAINS WERE POWERED BY PRESSURIZED STEAM FROM THE STEAM ENGINE. THIS STEAM WAS ALSO USED FOR THE BRAKES AND THE TRAIN WHISTLE.

Strong and gentle

The Victorians invented some amazing machines. In 1840, James Nasmyth designed a steam-driven hammer. The hammer was strong enough to bend iron bars, but it was also designed to do very delicate jobs. It could even crack an egg resting on a wine glass!

CITIES, TOWNS AND PORTS

Cities, towns and ports all expanded at an amazing rate. Growth was especially rapid in the Midlands and the North of England. The area around Birmingham was known as 'the black country' because of its metal foundries that belched out clouds of smoke. Manchester, Leeds and Bradford were major centres for cloth factories (often known as mills). Glasgow, Liverpool and Bristol were busy ports with huge shipbuilding yards.

BUILDING STEAMSHIPS REQUIRED VAST AMOUNTS OF COAL AND IRON, AS WELL AS SKILLED ENGINEERS AND A LARGE, CHEAP WORKFORCE.

FACTORIES AND MINES

In the early years of Victoria's reign, people often worked a thirteen-hour day in the factories and mines. They were very badly paid and many suffered terrible accidents.

CLOTH FACTORIES

Thousands of people were employed to operate the huge, noisy machines that spun cotton and wove it into cloth. It was tiring, dusty and dangerous work, but child-workers suffered even more. In the 1830s, factory owners often employed children as young as six years old. The children, known as 'scavengers', were forced to crawl under the weaving machines while they were still running. Many children lost their fingers in the machinery and some were even crushed to death.

OTHER JOBS IN INDUSTRY

As British industry grew, millions of jobs were created. Foundry workers sweated over furnaces to turn iron ore into iron and steel. Firemen and stokers kept the steam engines running. Britain's factory workers produced a vast range of goods, from cloth and carriages to matches and screws. There was also plenty of work laying railways, and building trains and ships.

DOWN THE MINES

Coal miners worked in long, narrow tunnels deep underground to dig up coal and iron ore. It was cold and damp inside the tunnels, and there was always the danger that a roof might collapse. Until the 1842 Mines Act, women and children worked in the mines with the men. Little children crouched by trap doors and held the doors open for carts carrying coal.

BOYS WORKING IN COAL MINES DRAGGED THE HEAVY COAL CARTS THROUGH DARK TUNNELS.

FACTORY ACTS

By the 1830s, some people were campaigning for changes in the workplace. They wanted better conditions for all working people, and they campaigned especially to protect children at work. Reformers like Lord Shaftesbury (see page 56) pressed the government to change the law, and gradually they got results. Between 1833 and 1891, the British government passed a series of Factory Acts. These acts reduced working hours and made it illegal for employers to hire children under ten years of age. The government also ruled that dangerous machinery should be fenced in. By the end of Victoria's reign, life had improved for most workers, although not all employers obeyed the law.

DIFFERENT CLASSES

The way people lived in Victorian times depended on their social class. If they belonged to the upper or middle classes, they could live very comfortably. If they were working class, their life was extremely hard. There were also some very poor people with no fixed work or home. They struggled to find enough food to eat or somewhere to sleep at night.

PEOPLE OF ALL CLASSES MINGLED ON THE BUSY CITY STREETS. THEY RANGED FROM UPPER-CLASS LADIES AND GENTLEMEN THROUGH TO CHIMNEY SWEEPS, STREET TRADERS AND THE HOMELESS.

FAMILY LIFE ACROSS THE CLASSES

Most upper-class families belonged to the aristocracy and did not need to work because they had inherited money. They lived in large houses in town with lots of servants and often had country homes as well.

Middle-class men generally worked as doctors, lawyers or army officers. These jobs paid a lot of money so their families could afford to live in comfort. The wives stayed at home and ran the house with the help of a few servants. Middle-class families usually lived in the suburbs, on the edge of the towns.

Working-class people worked extremely hard for very little money. Often, both parents went out to work and left the children to look after themselves. Working-class jobs included mining, building, carpentry and factory work, and some women worked as shop assistants or domestic servants. Families lived in crowded houses or rooms in the noisiest and dirtiest parts of town.

WORKHOUSES AND THE POOR

At the bottom of society were the very poor. After the Poor Law Amendment Act in 1834, they could only get help from the government by going to a workhouse.

It wasn't just the unemployed who ended up in workhouses – the old, ill, disabled or orphaned could be sent there, too. Families were split up and men, women and children were put in separate buildings. People were expected to work to pay for their keep, with long hours spent doing hard and boring jobs such as breaking up stones or unpicking ropes. Everyone had to wear a uniform and there was never enough to eat.

COUNTRY LIFE

Many country people worked on big farms that belonged to rich landowners. Farm workers were paid very low wages, most of which were spent on renting a cottage for their family. Farm workers looked after the animals, harvested crops, dug up vegetables and picked fruit. Women often worked as dairy maids, milking cows and making butter and cheese. Children were expected to help, too. Small children fed the chickens and pigs, and worked as bird-scarers in the fields.

BIRD-SCARERS SWUNG A NOISY RATTLE TO KEEP THE BIRDS AWAY FROM THE FARMER'S CROPS.

MACHINES TAKE OVER

In the 1850s, steam-powered tractors and threshing machines began to be used on farms. These new machines rapidly took over the farm workers' jobs and many people left to look for factory jobs in the towns instead.

TOWN LIFE

By the 1900s, over half of all British people lived in cities and towns. Britain had become an urban nation, but cities were often over-crowded and dirty. At the heart of the towns were enormous factories and crammed in close to them were hundreds of workers' houses. With so many people living close to each other, disease spread easily.

A TYPICALLY NARROW VICTORIAN STREET IN A WORKING-CLASS PART OF TOWN.

TRADERS AND SHOPS

City streets were filled with people trying to earn a living. Traders sold bread, milk and pies from carts. Girls stood on street corners with baskets of flowers or trays of matches for sale. Boys offered to shine shoes or run errands. Women sat in doorways selling a range of goods, from second-hand clothes to medicines and spices. Shopkeepers set up their businesses in the quieter streets. As well as the food shops, such as grocers, butchers and bakers, there were specialist shops, like drapers, selling cloth, and milliners, making hats.

Helping the Poor

As Britain grew richer, the lives of the poor became harder. Poor people suffered everywhere, but life was especially grim in the towns and cities. A few determined people decided that this suffering could not continue. Some of them campaigned for changes in the law and a number of brave workers began to stand up for their rights. Others set up charities to help the poor.

Dr Barnardo's homes

Dr Thomas Barnardo opened his first children's home in 1870. The home provided shelter, food and clothing for children whose parents had died or whose parents were too poor to look after them. Barnardo made sure that the children were educated, so they could find good jobs when they grew up. By the time of his death, in 1905, he had rescued nearly 100,000 children from the city streets.

THOMAS BARNARDO BELIEVED THAT EVERY CHILD DESERVED THE BEST POSSIBLE START IN LIFE.

THE SALVATION ARMY

In 1865, William and Catherine Booth founded the Salvation Army movement. Their aim was to help the poor and homeless, and spread the Christian religion. The Salvation Army set up mission houses to provide free shelter, food and clothing. They held public meetings with hymns and prayers, and offered help to anyone who needed it.

SALVATION ARMY OFFICERS WORE DISTINCTIVE UNIFORMS.

A VOICE FOR THE WORKERS

By the 1840s, working people had begun to form trade unions. These groups of workers demanded better pay, shorter working hours, and safer workplaces. When employers refused to listen to their demands, union leaders organized strikes. In 1892, a mining union leader called James Keir Hardie became the first working-class Member of Parliament. He set up the Labour Party to represent working people. (For other famous social reformers, see pages 56–57.)

A penny hang

Some homeless people were so desperate for a place to sleep that they paid for a 'penny hang'. They hung their arms and head over a thick rope and tried to get to sleep.

27

FAMILY LIFE

Victorian families were usually large. The average British family in the 1870s had five or six children. The father was the head of the household. He expected his wife and children to obey him without question.

CHILDREN

Boys and girls from wealthy families were often brought up by a nanny and spent most of their time in the nursery. Many children only saw their parents for a short while before they went to bed.

Working-class children were treated like small adults. They were expected to look after their younger brothers and sisters.

WEALTHY CHILDREN PLAYED, ATE AND SLEPT IN THEIR NURSERY.

Servants

In an upper-class home, the butler and the housekeeper were in charge of the staff. Other servants included a valet, who looked after the master's clothes, a lady's maid, a cook, a gardener and a groom to look after the horses.

BUTLER   VALET   COOK

HOUSEKEEPER   HOUSEMAID

DIFFERENT HOMES

Upper-class families lived in enormous houses with many rooms. Middle-class families had comfortable homes, with several bedrooms, a dining room, and a drawing room where the family sat together. The cook prepared the meals in a large basement kitchen. The servants slept in small rooms in the attic.

Homes for workers were built in long rows, or terraces. They were very small, with two rooms upstairs and a living room and kitchen downstairs. The houses had no bathroom and several families shared the same outside toilet. Some people lived in large buildings, called tenements, which were divided into many rooms.

A WEALTHY UPPER-CLASS FAMILY.

SOME POOR FAMILIES LIVED TOGETHER IN A SINGLE TENEMENT ROOM.

Bath time!

In homes with no bathroom, a tin bath was filled with hot water and put in front of the fire. The family took turns to wash in it. Sometimes up to twelve people used the same bathwater!

EDUCATION

Only a few children went to school in the early years of Victoria's reign. Wealthy parents sent their sons to expensive private schools, such as Eton and Harrow, while their daughters were tutored at home by a governess. Some parents sent their children to Sunday Schools, run by churches. But many poor families thought education was a waste of time.

In 1870, the British government passed the first Education Act. This marked the start of a series of laws that aimed to provide education for all. By the 1880s, elementary schools, for children aged five to ten, had been built across the country. In 1891, a law was passed to give free education to most children aged between five and thirteen.

CHILDREN IN GOVERNMENT SCHOOLS SAT AT DESKS IN CROWDED CLASSROOMS. THERE COULD BE UP TO SEVENTY PUPILS IN A CLASS AND ALL THEIR SUBJECTS WERE TAUGHT BY THE SAME TEACHER.

LESSON TIME

Victorian teachers concentrated on the basic subjects of reading, writing and arithmetic. There were also lessons in religion, history and geography, but most schools did not teach science. Pupils learnt to write by copying out passages from books. Young children wrote with chalk on a slate. Older ones had ink pens and copy books. In a maths lesson, pupils said their times tables out loud. For geography, they learnt the capital cities of all the countries in the British Empire.

School punishments

When the teacher asked a question, pupils had to stand up and give the correct answer. If they got the answer wrong, they had to stand in the corner of the schoolroom wearing a dunce's cap. Pupils who were naughty or late for school were struck with a ruler or beaten with a cane.

School sports

Boys at private schools played a range of sports, including cricket and rugby. Children in government schools had a lesson called drill. Pupils had to perform a set of strict exercises, such as marching or touching toes, while a teacher made sure they all kept time with each other.

HOLIDAYS

By the 1870s, the Industrial Revolution was in full swing in Britain and some people could afford to take holidays. The government introduced bank holidays, and most factories closed for a week in the summer. Many people travelled by rail to the seaside. Poorer families took a working holiday in the country, doing farm jobs such as fruit-picking.

BESIDE THE SEASIDE

Seaside holiday-makers enjoyed strolling along the promenade, visiting shopping arcades and listening to brass bands. There were puppet shows and donkey rides on the beach, and entertainments on the pier. People arrived at the beach fully clothed. Then they changed into their bathing costumes in a bathing hut, which was wheeled into the sea to prevent anyone seeing them!

A BUSY SEASIDE RESORT IN VICTORIAN TIMES

LEISURE

As well as reading books, papers and magazines at home, the Victorians played the piano and sang popular songs. Adults and children played chess, cards and dominoes, and families and friends took part in lively games of forfeits and charades.

People living in towns had a wide choice of entertainment. Wealthy couples went to concerts and plays. Working-class people saved up for an evening at a music hall. Music hall shows combined comedy acts with song and dance routines, and people sang along to some of the songs. People in the countryside had fewer entertainments, but they still looked forward to regular visits from travelling fairs and circuses.

Sport was very popular in Victorian times. People played tennis and football, and went cycling in the country. Football stadiums were built in towns and cities, and huge crowds gathered to support their local team.

CLOTHES AND FASHION

By the start of Queen Victoria's reign, most people wore factory-made clothes. Poor people, though, had ragged, second-hand clothes and many poor parents could not even afford to buy shoes for their children.

WOMEN'S STYLES

The shape of women's dresses altered several times in the Victorian period as fashions changed.

1850s
Crinolines were large, hooped frames, worn under dresses instead of petticoats to make skirts look as wide and full as possible.

1870s
Bustles were pads that held up the skirt in a shelf at the back. Some were stuffed with horsehair or straw while others were made of steel.

Cruel corsets

Underneath their dresses, women wore corsets, laced up very tightly to make their waists look as tiny as possible. Corsets were made from cotton, with steel or whalebone 'stays' stitched into panels. They were very painful to wear.

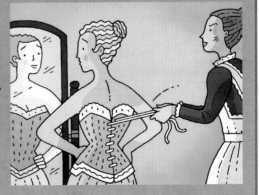

MEN'S STYLES

A WEALTHY MAN

Black silk
top hat

Frock coat worn
with a high-collared
shirt and waistcoat
underneath

Gloves

Walking stick

A WORKING MAN

Bowler hat

Short jacket,
also with a
waistcoat and
shirt underneath

Trousers worn
with short,
ankle-length boots

Mutton chops

Victorian men kept their hair short, but
many men grew beards, moustaches
and sideburns. Some men's sideburns
covered large parts of their face. They
were nicknamed 'mutton chops'.

CHILDREN'S CLOTHES

Unlike children today,
Victorian boys and
girls generally wore
smaller versions of
adults' clothes.

Until they were around
four years old, boys
and girls looked very
much the same. They
both wore long, loose
dresses and had their
hair curled.

FOOD AND DRINK

Until the 1800s, most people in Britain ate food they had grown themselves or that was produced by local farmers. But this way of life changed during Victoria's reign. Instead, people in towns bought their food from shops or from traders in the streets. They had more variety in their diet, although their food was not always fresh or healthy.

FOOD FROM NEAR AND FAR

Some of the food sold in shops came from local farmers and some was transported by train and ship. Items like rice and tea were imported from distant parts of the Empire. Fresh food did not last long as there were no refrigerators, so families ate a lot of bottled and pickled foods. Canned foods appeared in the shops in the 1850s and in time became very popular.

A VICTORIAN GROCER'S SHOP SOLD JUST ABOUT EVERYTHING!

DIFFERENT DIETS

Wealthy people enjoyed a rich and varied diet, including different meats, shellfish and cheeses. They ate exotic foreign fruits, such as peaches, pineapples and grapes. Even middle-class families ate meat or fish every day, as well as fruit, vegetables, bread, butter, eggs and jam. But not everyone was so lucky. Some poor families often ate nothing but bread soaked in milk. Others survived mainly on porridge and potatoes, though low-quality meat such as 'broxy' (meat from diseased sheep) was sometimes available.

Unhealthy food

Not all the food on sale was very nice. Some bakers added chalk to their flour. Dishonest grocers mixed shavings of wood with their tea. In the 1840s, an ice-cream making machine was invented. Ice-cream was sold on city streets as a great treat, but it often contained human and animal hairs, and even lice and beetles!

Heads and feet

Cooks tried to use all the parts of an animal, including its head and feet! Pig's trotters and calf's head were common dishes, and people often ate cooked brains and tongue.

Pudding please!

Wealthy Victorians liked to end every meal with a pudding. Favourites were bread-and-butter pudding, jam roly-poly and spotted dick (a sponge pudding with currants).

TRAVEL AND TRANSPORT

In Victoria's reign, Britain was gripped by 'railway madness'. By the 1850s, the country was covered with a network of railway lines and, by the end of the century, cars and buses had also arrived.

TRAVEL BY RAIL

Trains first began to take passengers in the 1820s and by the 1840s the idea of passenger trains had really taken off. Many people took the train to work, and families travelled by rail to visit relatives or go on holiday. The world's first underground train line opened in London in 1863. At first the trains were pulled by steam engines, and passengers travelled underground in open wagons! In the 1890s, steam engines were replaced by electric motors. By this time, people were travelling in covered carriages.

A BUSY VICTORIAN TRAIN PLATFORM.

WAIT HERE FOR THIRD CLASS

WAY OUT

HORSELESS CARRIAGES

At the start of the Victorian age, travel by road depended on horses. People went on horseback, or rode in horse-drawn carriages or buses. Then, in the 1880s, cars with petrol engines began to appear. These early motorcars were known as 'horseless carriages'. By the 1890s, brand-new motor buses had started to replace the horse-drawn buses. At the same time, electric trams were introduced. Trams ran on rails set into the roads and their power was delivered through overhead cables.

Waving the flag

When motor cars were first invented, the government passed a law known as the Red Flag Act. All vehicles with engines had to drive behind a man with a red flag. The man walked along the road, waving his red flag to warn people that a car was coming!

Boneshakers

In the 1860s, people started using bicycles. The first bicycles were known as 'boneshakers' because they were so painful to ride. The safety bicycle was invented in 1885. The forerunner of today's bicycles, it was much easier to ride than the early models.

THE BUILDING BOOM

During the Victorian period, houses, churches, schools and factories were built in towns and cities all over Britain. Architects designed grand public buildings, and engineers worked on railways, roads and canals. This massive building boom did not just happen in Britain – buildings and railways were constructed all over the British Empire.

VICTORIAN STYLE

Victorian architects took most of their ideas from the buildings of the past. They were especially impressed by the castles and churches of the Middle Ages. Many Victorian buildings are built in a medieval style, with pointed roofs and turrets. Some buildings were based on Ancient Greek and Roman temples and a few were even inspired by Ancient Egyptian styles.

TOWER BRIDGE IN LONDON TOOK EIGHT YEARS TO BUILD AND WAS COMPLETED IN 1894. ITS TWIN TOWERS LOOK LIKE MEDIEVAL CASTLES.

GLASS AND IRON

Victorian builders discovered a new way of building using plate-glass panels set in a framework of iron bars. They used this method to build enormous structures that were strong and light. Many railway stations today still have Victorian roofs made from glass and iron. The biggest building made from these materials was the Crystal Palace, which was built to house the Great Exhibition of 1851 (see pages 44-45).

AMAZING ENGINEERING

The most outstanding engineer of the Victorian age was Isambard Kingdom Brunel. He created the Great Western Railway, which ran from London to Bristol. This enormous task involved designing the engines, the railway track, the stations, the bridges and the tunnels. Brunel also worked on a tunnel under the River Thames, and designed a famous steamship, called the SS *Great Britain*.

Tunnel terror!

Box Tunnel, on the Great Western Railway line, is one of Brunel's greatest achievements. It measures nearly two miles long and it took five years to build. When it was finished, in 1841, it was the longest railway tunnel in the world. At first, some passengers were too scared to ride through it. Instead, they took a carriage to the other end of the tunnel, where they joined the train again!

INVENTIONS AND IDEAS

Victorian scientists made some very important discoveries. Telephones and electric lights, for example, were used for the first time by the Victorians. Queen Victoria's reign was also a time of exciting new ideas. Some of these ideas changed the way that people saw the world.

Electric lights

In the 1830s, the British scientist Michael Faraday discovered a way to produce electricity. Then, in the 1870s, the light bulb was invented by Joseph Swan in Britain and Thomas Edison in the USA. By the 1880s, electric street lights had begun to replace the old gas lamps, but only very wealthy homes had their own electric lights.

Telegraphs and telephones

In 1837, the electric telegraph was invented. It worked by sending electrical signals down a wire cable. This discovery led to another invention. In 1876, Alexander Graham Bell, a Scotsman living in the USA, demonstrated the first telephone. The first words spoken down a telephone line were: "Mr Watson, come here. I want to see you."

Cameras

Photography was discovered in the 1820s, but some important developments were made in Victorian times. In 1840, William Henry Fox Talbot invented a new way of taking photographs. He used specially treated paper, which could be turned into photographic prints. Fox Talbot also created a small box camera. This made photography much easier than before.

The theory of evolution

In 1859, the scientist Charles Darwin published a very important book, called *On the Origin of Species*. It stated that all forms of life on Earth had evolved over millions of years rather than being created by God in seven days. People were especially shocked by the idea that human beings were descended from apes.

An early computer

The British mathematician, Charles Babbage, is often described as the inventor of the computer. He worked for many years on a giant calculating machine. The machine was designed to follow simple programs, which took the form of large cards with holes punched in them. Ada Lovelace worked with Babbage and prepared the cards for his calculating machine.

THE GREAT EXHIBITION

The Great Exhibition of 1851 was one of the high points of Victoria's reign. It was organized by Prince Albert 'to celebrate the industry of all nations'. Albert's special aim was to show off British inventions. He wanted people from all over the world to buy British products and boost British industry.

The exhibition was held in Hyde Park, London, inside a massive building known as the Crystal Palace. Objects on display ranged from giant steam engines to delicate microscopes. One of the most exciting areas to visit was the Hall of Machines in Motion that contained examples of the latest factory machinery. Visitors from all classes marvelled at the range of British products and inventions, and wealthy businessmen placed large orders.

Free London museums

Prince Albert used the profits from the Great Exhibition to set up the museum now called the Victoria and Albert Museum (this included the collections that now make up the Science and Natural History museums). Entrance was free so people of all classes could enjoy the displays.

GREAT EXHIBITION FACTS

• The Crystal Palace covered an area the size of four football pitches.

• After the exhibition, the Crystal Palace was taken down and rebuilt in a park in south London. It burnt down in 1936.

• Exotic exhibits included a stuffed elephant from India, and an enormous diamond from South Africa.

• The central hall of the Crystal Palace had to be tall enough to fit some enormous trees that were growing where it was built!

• 250,000 people bought a season ticket so they could visit the exhibition many times.

• Queen Victoria and her family made a total of thirteen visits!

• Some inventions on display were very unusual. They included a giant penknife with eighty different blades and a folding piano.

IN THE SIX MONTHS IT WAS OPEN, THE GREAT EXHIBITION WAS VISITED BY OVER SIX MILLION PEOPLE.

HEALTH AND MEDICINE

Victorian towns and cities were very unhealthy places – especially for the poor. Factory chimneys belched out smoke. The streets were filled with rotting food. Drains and sewers often overflowed and the rivers were polluted. This pollution led to frequent outbreaks of deadly diseases like cholera and typhoid, which spread rapidly through the crowded, dirty streets. Other serious diseases such as smallpox, measles and tuberculosis were all passed easily from one person to another. Many working-class people were already weak and ill, so they died in very large numbers. Children were especially likely to die.

IN THE SUMMER OF 1858, THE RIVER THAMES IN LONDON BECAME SO POLLUTED THAT PEOPLE HAD TO KEEP THEIR MOUTHS AND NOSES COVERED. THE RIVER'S DISGUSTING SMELL WAS CALLED 'THE GREAT STINK'.

Cleaning up the towns

During Queen Victoria's reign, the government took some serious steps to improve hygiene. New sewage pipes were laid, streets were cleaned and rubbish was collected. Slowly, the rivers became less polluted and water became safer to drink.

Horrible hospitals

Hospitals in the 1830s were messy, dirty and full of germs. Doctors did not wash their hands or their instruments, so infection spread fast. Operations were carried out without an anaesthetic to put the patient to sleep. Many people died from shock during the operation or soon afterwards.

Children at risk

Some children did jobs that put their health at risk every day. Chimney sweeps were forced to climb up narrow chimneys. They suffered serious cuts, bruises and burns. Some boys fell to their death or were suffocated by falling soot.

Making changes

Fortunately, hospital care improved in the second half of the 1800s. In 1847, chloroform gas, a form of anaesthetic, began to be used in hospitals. In 1865, Joseph Lister invented an antiseptic spray to kill germs.

CRIME AND PUNISHMENT

All sorts of criminals lurked in the cities. Gangs of boys worked as pickpockets. Armed burglars stole from shops and houses. Some criminals were violent and cruel, but many did not mean any harm. They were simply desperate for food.

PUNISHMENTS AND PRISONS

Punishments for crimes were very harsh. People who had simply stolen a loaf of bread could be whipped in public or sent to prison. Some people who had committed minor crimes were sent away to Australia in convict ships. Murderers were sentenced to death by hanging. Hangings took place in public until 1868 and large crowds gathered to watch.

Victorian prisons were terrifying places. Prisoners had very little to eat and had to do hard but pointless work, such as walking round and round on a wooden treadmill. Some prisoners lived in old warships, known as 'hulks', that were moored in the River Thames.

PRISONERS ON SHIPS WORE LEG-IRONS AT ALL TIMES TO STOP THEM JUMPING OVERBOARD.

NEW POLICE

In 1829, the first police force was founded in London by Sir Robert Peel. The detective branch of the police force, whose job was to solve crimes, was formed in 1842.

Bobbies on the beat

Policemen were nicknamed 'bobbies' or 'peelers' after Sir Robert Peel. London bobbies walked the city streets, looking out for trouble. Bobbies wore top hats and tailcoats until 1860. Then they started wearing tunics and helmets.

Jack the Ripper

In 1888, five women were murdered in the East End of London. Their killer was nicknamed 'Jack the Ripper'. The police never discovered who Jack the Ripper really was.

Snow droppers

Thieves called snow droppers snatched clothes from washing lines and sold them on again!

THE ARTS

WRITERS

In the Victorian period, more people learned to read than ever before. There was a huge demand for stories and news. Publishers used steam-powered printing presses to keep up with the public demand for things to read. They produced books, papers and magazines very cheaply.

Charles Dickens

Dickens was one of the most popular Victorian novelists and many of his fifteen novels were published first as serials in magazines. He was a talented performer and often gave dramatic readings of his work.

The Brontë sisters

Anne, Emily and Charlotte Brontë all wrote best-selling novels. Charlotte was the author of four novels including *Jane Eyre*. Her sister Emily wrote *Wuthering Heights* and Anne wrote *The Tenant of Wildfell Hall*.

Children's books

The Victorian period was a great time for children's books. In 1865, Lewis Carroll published *Alice's Adventures in Wonderland*. Then came *Treasure Island* by Robert Louis Stevenson and *The Jungle Book* by Rudyard Kipling.

PAINTERS

The Victorians loved paintings that told a story. Some artists painted sad pictures of sick children. Others showed romantic scenes, with castles and mountains. One group of artists, called the Pre-Raphaelites, was inspired by the art of the Middle Ages. They painted scenes of knights and ladies, based on the legends of King Arthur.

PHOTOGRAPHERS

Before the Victorian period, only wealthy people had their portraits painted. But the invention of photography led to a new kind of portrait. Photographers were kept very busy taking pictures of families and couples. Julia Margaret Cameron was one of the first Victorian photographers. She was famous for her artistic portraits of writers and artists.

Penny dreadfuls

'Penny dreadfuls' were magazines that came out once a week and cost one penny. They were packed full of stories of mystery and romance. Many people loved them, but the more educated Victorians thought they were badly written and 'dreadful'!

Not amused?

In most Victorian photographs, people look very solemn. This was because they had to stay completely still for several minutes when they posed for a photograph. If they moved, the picture would be blurred.

THE END OF AN ERA

Queen Victoria reigned for almost sixty four years. She was not always popular, but many people grew to respect her.

In 1887, there were great celebrations to mark her Golden Jubilee (fifty years on the throne). Ten years later, the British people celebrated again, holding parades and street parties for the Diamond Jubilee. Queen Victoria is one of only two British monarchs in history to have reached the milestone of sixty years on the throne (the other is Queen Elizabeth II).

To celebrate her Diamond Jubilee, Queen Victoria was driven through the streets of London in an open carriage. She later wrote in her diary: 'The crowds were quite indescribable and their enthusiasm truly marvellous and deeply touching'.

THE QUEEN'S LAST YEARS

By the time of her Diamond Jubilee in 1897, Victoria was a frail old lady of seventy eight. She had very bad eyesight and had to be pushed around in a wheelchair.

Meanwhile, the British government faced a number of problems. Many people in Britain lived in great poverty and the government struggled to keep control of its massive empire. Britain was losing its position as world leader and the USA and Germany were the new industrial powers. There was also trouble in Ireland, with violent protests against English rule.

A ROYAL FUNERAL

On 22 January 1901, Queen Victoria died at Osborne House, on the Isle of Wight. Her funeral took place at Windsor and she was buried beside her beloved Prince Albert. Victoria was succeeded by her oldest son, Albert Edward. Many people were sad to see the end of the Victorian era, but they also looked forward to having King Edward VII on the throne. The period of Edward's reign later become known as the Edwardian era.

Grandmother of Europe
Queen Victoria was known as the Grandmother of Europe. Her children had married members of all the major royal families in Europe, and had many children of their own. In total, she had forty two grandchildren and eighty five great-grandchildren!

WHAT THE VICTORIANS DID FOR US

The Victorian era is sometimes called the start of the modern age. Once you start to look around, you can see signs of the Victorians everywhere. In fact, it is impossible to imagine our lives today without Victorian buildings, transport and inventions.

Railways and buildings

Victorian railway stations, bridges and tunnels are still used every day in parts of the world.

Many people today still live in Victorian-built homes, although a Victorian family would have a shock if they saw inside!

Some of London's most famous buildings were designed and built by the Victorians. Who can imagine London without Tower Bridge, the Houses of Parliament or Big Ben?

Great stories

Victorian writers were great storytellers, and people still enjoy their books. *Oliver Twist*, *Jane Eyre* and *Alice in Wonderland* are just a few of the brilliant Victorian stories that remain popular today.

Fun and games

Did you know that before Victorian times, people didn't send Christmas cards or pull crackers? They were invented by the Victorians! The Victorians also introduced the idea of a seaside holiday. They were the first people to build seaside piers and have mobile ice-cream sellers.

Great inventions

Next time you use a phone, a camera or a computer, you can thank the Victorians! It was their inventions that laid the foundations for our modern technology. When you make a journey, you can thank them again. Bicycles, cars and underground trains all appeared for the first time in the Victorian age.

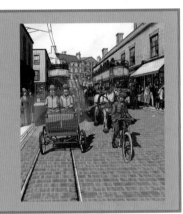

Useful inventions

The Victorians invented many useful items, such as postage stamps that we now take for granted. The 'Penny Black' was the world's first stamp. Issued in 1840, it cost one penny, hence its name.

Flushing toilets were in use before Victorian times, but in the 1880s Thomas Crapper made popular a model that could be installed in any home.

Other Victorian inventions are lawn mowers, matches and chocolate bars!

Penny Black

toilet

chocolate bar

IMPORTANT VICTORIANS

The Victorian age produced some outstanding men and women. Gladstone and Disraeli, Dickens and Darwin, Florence Nightingale and Isambard Kingdom Brunel are names that are still recognized all over the world. Some of the people on these pages are not as famous as these great figures, but they all made a difference to Victorian life.

ADA LOVELACE
(1815-1852)
A scientist and mathematician who worked with Charles Babbage on his calculating machine. Often called 'the first computer programmer', her work helped to create the first modern computers.

ELIZABETH GARRETT ANDERSON
(1836-1917)
The first woman in England to qualify as a doctor and a surgeon. In 1872, she founded the New Hospital for Women in London, which had an all-female staff. She was also an active member of the suffragette movement.

LORD SHAFTESBURY
(1801-1885)
Anthony Ashley Cooper, usually known as Lord Shaftesbury, was a Member of Parliament who helped to pass a series of laws to improve the lives of working children. He was also the chairman of the Ragged School Union, an organization that set up over a hundred schools for poor children.

OCTAVIA HILL
(1838-1912)

A campaigner for social reform, she organized the building of social housing for homeless families and was also one of the founders of the National Trust.

WILLIAM MORRIS
(1834-1896)

A designer, artist, writer and founder of the Arts and Crafts movement. He also campaigned for better conditions for working people. Today, he is best known for his designs for curtains and wallpaper.

TITUS SALT
(1803-1876)

A factory owner who believed that workers should have good working and living conditions. He constructed the model village of Saltaire in Bradford for his workers.

JOSEPH LISTER
(1827-1912)

A surgeon who realized that it was very important to kill germs in wounds. He introduced the use of carbolic acid as an antiseptic spray. This led to a dramatic drop in the number of deaths in British hospitals.

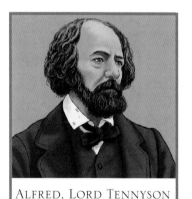

ALFRED, LORD TENNYSON
(1809-1892)

One of the greatest Victorian poets, with famous poems including *The Lady of Shallott* and *The Charge of the Light Brigade*. He became Poet Laureate in 1850, succeeding William Wordsworth.

ISABELLA BEETON
(1836-1865)

Author of the famous guide, *Mrs Beeton's Book of Household Management*. The book had over 1,112 pages, with over 900 pages of recipes, and was an instant best-seller. By 1868 it had sold nearly two million copies.

Timeline

1837   Victoria becomes Queen of the United Kingdom of Great Britain and Ireland at the age of eighteen.
The electric telegraph is invented.
Charles Dickens publishes the first instalment of *Oliver Twist*.

1838   The London to Birmingham railway line opens, marking the start of a railway-building boom.

1839   William Henry Fox Talbot demonstrates a new way of taking photographs.

1840   Queen Victoria marries Prince Albert.
The 'Penny Post' is introduced, marking the start of an efficient postal system.

1841   The Great Western Railway is completed, under the direction of engineer Isambard Kingdom Brunel.

1842   The Mines Act ends child labour in mines.

1844   The Factories Act is introduced, reducing working hours for children aged nine to thirteen years.

1845   Brunel completes the steamship SS *Great Britain*.

1847   Chloroform gas is first used as an anaesthetic in operations.
A Factory Act passed, reducing a working day to ten hours.
Emily Brontë publishes *Wuthering Heights*.
Charlotte Brontë publishes *Jane Eyre*.

1848   The Pre-Raphaelite group of artists is formed.
Cholera epidemic in London leads to Public Health Acts.

1850   Dickens publishes *David Copperfield*.

1851   The Great Exhibition is held in London.

1853   The Crimean War begins.

1854   Florence Nightingale goes to the Crimea to organize nursing.

1856   The Crimean War ends.

1857   The Indian Mutiny begins.

1858   The British government takes control of India.
'The great stink' overpowers London.

1859   Charles Darwin publishes *On the Origin of Species*, outlining his theory of evolution.

1861 PRINCE ALBERT DIES, AGED FORTY TWO.

THE AMERICAN CIVIL WAR BEGINS.

1863 THE WORLD'S FIRST UNDERGROUND TRAIN SYSTEM OPENS IN LONDON.

1865 THE AMERICAN CIVIL WAR ENDS.

LEWIS CARROLL PUBLISHES *ALICE'S ADVENTURES IN WONDERLAND*.

WILLIAM AND CATHERINE BOOTH FOUND THE SALVATION ARMY MOVEMENT.

1867 JOSEPH LISTER INTRODUCES ANTISEPTICS IN HOSPITALS.

THE NATIONAL SOCIETY FOR WOMEN'S SUFFRAGE IS FORMED TO
CAMPAIGN FOR VOTES FOR WOMEN.

1868 BENJAMIN DISRAELI BECOMES PRIME MINISTER FOR THE FIRST TIME.
HE IS DEFEATED NINE MONTHS LATER.

WILLIAM EWART GLADSTONE BECOMES PRIME MINISTER FOR THE
FIRST TIME.

1870 DR THOMAS BARNARDO OPENS HIS FIRST CHILDREN'S HOME
IN LONDON.

1876 SCOTTISH INVENTOR ALEXANDER GRAHAM BELL DEMONSTRATES
THE FIRST TELEPHONE.

QUEEN VICTORIA IS DECLARED EMPRESS OF INDIA.

1878 ELECTRIC LAMPS ARE DEMONSTRATED IN BRITAIN BY JOSEPH SWAN.

1879 THOMAS EDISON DEVELOPS A MORE PRACTICAL FORM OF THE ELECTRIC
LIGHT BULB IN THE USA.

1880 THE EDUCATION ACT MAKES IT COMPULSORY FOR CHILDREN TO GO
TO SCHOOL.

THE FIRST BOER WAR BEGINS

1885 GERMAN ENGINEER KARL BENZ BUILDS THE FIRST MOTOR CAR.

THE SAFETY BICYCLE IS INVENTED.

1888 JACK THE RIPPER COMMITS A SERIES OF MURDERS IN LONDON.

1891 THE ELEMENTARY EDUCATION ACT PROVIDES FUNDING FOR ALL
CHILDREN AGED BETWEEN FOUR AND FOURTEEN TO GO TO SCHOOL.

1893 NEW ZEALAND IS THE FIRST COUNTRY TO GIVE WOMEN
THE RIGHT TO VOTE.

1895 ITALIAN INVENTOR GUGLIELMO MARCONI INVENTS THE RADIO.

1899 THE SECOND BOER WAR BEGINS IN SOUTH AFRICA. IT LASTS UNTIL 1902.

1901 QUEEN VICTORIA DIES, AGED 81. SHE IS SUCCEEDED BY HER
SON KING EDWARD VII.

GLOSSARY

antiseptic a substance that kills or prevents the growth and spread of germs

architect someone who designs and oversees the construction of buildings

aristocracy the highest class in society

bales bundles of goods, such as cotton or paper

campaign a series of actions organized to strive for a particular result

child labour the use of children in hard physical work

cotton soft, white material from a plant that can be spun into cloth

Diamond Jubilee the sixtieth anniversary of a king or queen's coronation

drill a regular physical or mental exercise

elementary school a school for children aged five to ten

empire a group of countries under a single ruler

engineer a person who designs, builds and maintains engines and machinery

exhibition a public display of works of art, items of interest or particular skills

foundry a factory that makes metal items

furnace a place used for heating materials to a very high temperature

Golden Jubilee the fiftieth anniversary of a king or queen's coronation

governess someone who teaches children in a private home instead of at school

import	to bring in goods from abroad
industry	manfacturing goods
knickerbockers	a type of baggy-kneed trousers
leg-irons	metal bands or chains placed around a prisoner's ankles to restrain them
loom	a machine used to weave thread or yarn
merchant	a buyer or seller of goods
missionaries	people sent to promote religion in other countries
Parliament	a group of people, including the ruling sovereign, responsible for making the laws of a country
pickpockets	people who steal from others' pockets
pier	a raised structure leading out from the shore into the water
pinafore	a sleeveless garment, a bit like an apron, worn over a dress
pollution	substances harmful or poisonous to the environment
port	where ships load or unload cargo
Prime Minister	the head and chief office of an elected government
promenade	a public place for walking, typically along a waterfront
rebellion	opposition and resistance to an authority
reformer	an individual who works for the improvement of an existing situation

Glossary

safety bicycle	a bicycle that has two wheels of equal size
serial	a series of stories or plays appearing regularly in magazines or newspapers
sewage	human waste and water carried in sewers
slate	a smooth, flat piece of stone that could be written on with chalk then wiped clean
stays	boning that made a woman's corset stiff and rigid
suburb	the outer edge of a town or city
suffragette	a woman fighting for the right to vote
threshing machine	machine used for separating grain or seeds from straw
trade unions	organizations formed by workers in a particular trade to protect their rights and interests
tutor	a private teacher who typically teaches single or small groups of students
typhoid	a disease that is usually passed from one person to another through dirty food and water
urban	relating to a town or city
workhouse	a place where the poor and needy worked in return for a place to eat and sleep